Winston Groom, the author of *Forrest Gump*, also wrote the acclaimed Vietnam War novel *Better Times Than These* as well as the prize-winning *As Summers ...* and co-authored *C... ... ...my*, whi... ... ... 1984 Pulitzer Priz... ... ...rk City and Point C... Alab...

Also by Winston Groom

FORREST GUMP

and published by Black Swan

Gumpisms

The Wit and Wisdom of Forrest Gump

WINSTON GROOM

CORGI BOOKS

GUMPisms
A CORGI BOOK : 0 552 14321 9

First publication in Great Britain

PRINTING HISTORY
Corgi edition published 1994

Corgi Books are published by Transworld Publishers Ltd,
61–63 Uxbridge Road, Ealing, London W5 5SA,
in Australia by Transworld Publishers (Australia) Pty Ltd,
15–25 Helles Avenue, Moorebank, NSW 2170,
and in New Zealand by Transworld Publishers (NZ) Ltd,
3 William Pickering Drive, Albany, Auckland.

Printed in Great Britain by
Mackays of Chatham, plc, Chatham, Kent.

Introduction

by P. J. O'Rourke

In Forrest Gump, Winston Groom created the ideal citizen for the modern world—a perfect idiot.

But there is a world of difference between being dumb and being wrong. Think of the most moronic things you have ever said. No doubt they fell mostly into the categories of "I hate you," "I love you," "I need another drink," and "I quit." These may have been unintelligent statements, but were they incorrect? Forrest isn't wrong much, either.

Now think about the most imbecilic things that have ever been done on earth—the Cultural Revolution in China, World War I,

"Beverly Hills 90210." Every one of them was done by smart people. There's a world of difference between smart and worth-a-damn, too.

We should never hesitate to listen to a fool about life because life is pretty foolish as far as I can tell. And the great thing about hearing from a birdbrain is that we can all understand what he's saying. Here's a quote from a well-known genius:

The mass of the sun curves space-time in such a way that although the earth follows a straight path in four-dimensional space-time, it appears to move along a circular orbit in three-dimensional space.
—Stephen W. Hawking,
A *Brief History of Time*

Can you understand that? Me neither. Here is a quote from Forrest Gump:

Do not try to cut your own hair.

People outsmart themselves all the time, but you can't practice self-deception if you're so dull-witted that you always see right through everything you're doing. Or, as Forrest says:

> Some people, like me, are born idiots, but many more become stupider as they go along.

~~~~~~~~

Let
me say this:
bein' an idiot
is no box
of chocolates.

~~~~~~~~

~~~~~~~~~

Nobody
ever got
into trouble
by keepin'
his mouth
shut.

~~~~~~~~~

~~~~~~~~~~

People not to talk back to:

1. Your teacher
2. 1st Sergeants
3. The police
4. Your mama

~~~~~~~~~~

Do not try to cut your own hair.

~~~~~~~~~~

Dream, but don't quit your day job.

~~~~~~~~~~~

If you
see a line,
go stand in it.
Probably
can't hurt
nothin'.

~~~~~~~~~~~

~~~~~~~~

Don't
own nothin'
if you can help it.
If you can,
even rent
your shoes.

~~~~~~~~

~~~~~~

If you want
to wear a hat,
do it in
the privacy
of your own
home.

~~~~~~

~~~~~~~~~~

Never trust
nobody that says
he never took
a drink
in his whole
life.

~~~~~~~~~~

Don't ever
pick a fight
with somebody
that's really
ugly-lookin'.

~~~~~~~~~

If you want to
be popular, do not
engage in child
molestin'
or line dancin'.

~~~~~~~~~

~~~~~~~~~~

Always save
enough money for
one phone call
and one use
of a pay toilet.

~~~~~~~~~~

If you can't sing good,
sing loud.

~~~~~~~~~

Do not
cry over
skim milk.

Don't
lick nothin'
that sticks
to your
tongue.

~~~~~~~~~~

Keep your
bullshit detector
in good
workin' order.

If you go
to the zoo,
always take somethin'
to feed the animals—
even if the signs say
"Do Not Feed
Animals."
It wasn't the animals
that put them signs up.

~~~~~~~~~~

Try to eat somethin'
bitter every day, just
so's
you don't lose
your taste
for it.

~~~~~~~~~~

~~~~~~~~~~

When you think
you're so low you gotta
look up to look down,
beat yourself hard on
the foot with a stick
for a while.
At least you will feel
better when
you stop.

~~~~~~~~~~

~~~~~~~~~~

Always be
ready to take
a chance:
look what it did
for Rocky.

~~~~~~~~~~

If you are ahead, shut up and stay there.

~~~~~~~~~~

A lot is to be said for the word *no*.

~~~~~~~~~~

Don't expect
anybody else
to help you.
If they do, fine.
If they don't,
file it away.

~~~~~~~~~~

~~~~~~~~~

Try not
to screw up.
This will satisfy
a few people,
and amaze
everybody else.

~~~~~~~~~

Remember this:
while somebody
is down there
kissin' your butt,
they could just
as easily
be bitin' it,
too.

~~~~~~~~~~

Put
Tabasco sauce on
everythin' you eat:
this way, you can
eat very cheap.

~~~~~~~~~~

Whatever
you do,
try to have
a reason to do it.

~~~~~~~~~~~~

There are
times when you
cannot let
the right thing
stand in your way.

To each,
his own ca-ca
smells sweet—
but do not
be fooled by this.

~~~~~~~~~~

Do not
drink soup;
it puts a lake
in your stomach.

Do not
ever roll dice
with a guy
called "Bones."

~~~~~~~~~~

You may be
an idiot,
but try not
to be *stupid*.

D

o not suck
your thumb—
or anybody else's,
for that matter.

When you are born under the wrong star, it will shine upon your butt forever— even while you are seated.

~~~~~~~~~~

Forget
"Don't get mad—
get even."
If you're really
mad, go ahead
and stomp that
sucker flat!

~~~~~~~~~~

~~~~~~~~~

If you
got to pee,
do not talk about it.
Just do it. Might not be
time later.

~~~~~~~~~

Do not play
the piano with jelly
on your fingers.
Also,
do not play
the saxophone
with jelly
in your mouth.

Always
be nice
to your
mama.

~~~~~~~~~~~

Most
people don't
look dumb
till they start
talkin'.

Remember this:
peace of mind
over piece of ass.

~~~~~~~~~~

Be very
suspicious if
somebody says they
want to make
a movie of your
life story.

Do not eat
anything you
do not know
what it is.

~~~~~~~~~~

You
got to cry,
do it by yourself,
and be quick
about it.

~~~~~~~~~~~~

Be prepared to
take some shit
in life; just do
not take more than
a mouthful at
a time.

~~~~~~~~~~~~

Beware
of people that
put numbers
after their names.

~~~~~~~~~~~

Do not park
in a space
that says
"Reserved for
Sheriff's Deputies."

~~~~~~~~~~

Do not put
stock in newspapers;
you can find out
more just by lookin'
around at what
is goin' on.

~~~~~~~~~~

~~~~~~~~~

Life is like
a rubber band;
harder you go
forward, harder you
snap back. So do
not make slip-ups.

~~~~~~~~~

~~~~~~

When you feel
there is an unfair
burden on your
shoulders, that's
just the way
it is sometimes.

~~~~~~

Always try to
do the right thing,
unless your
conscience tells
you otherwise.

~~~~~~~~~~

To save energy,
do not go out
lookin' for trouble;
chances are, it will
find you soon enough.

~~~~~~~~~~

A beggar is
no different
than you or me,
'cept he ain't
got no money.
Always keep
some spare change
to give a beggar.

~~~~~~~~~~

~~~~~~~~~

Do not cuss,
holler, pee, or throw up
in public places
or otherwise call
attention to yourself,
as it will probably
get you in trouble.

~~~~~~~~~

41

Two rules:
do not never
paint houses
or move furniture.

~~~~~~~~~~

Whenever you can,
take the train—
providin' you ain't
got to be nowhere
on time.

A
lways say
"thank you,"
even if you
don't mean it.

~~~~~~~~~~~

D
o not
make excuses
unless
you have to.

You can catch
more flies with honey
than you can
with vinegar,
but you can also
catch more flies
with garbage than
either of them
other two—assumin'
you are into
catchin' flies.

If you're gonna
screw up, do it
while you are young.
Older you get,
harder it is
to bounce back.

When the
shit is about
to hit the fan,
do *somethin'*—
even if it
is wrong.

~~~~~~~~

Don't try to
outrun nobody
if you're
wearin' sandals.

Never mix water with chocolate.

~~~~~~~~~~

Do not get drunk around strangers.

If you have
to make a choice
between a clean
mind and a clean
body, it oughtn't
to be no contest.

~~~~~~~~~

Whenever
somebody says
"I am here to
help you,"
hold on to
your wallet.

~~~~~~~~~

~~~~~~~~~~

Life can be
one big toilet,
so for all our
sakes, don't
make waves.

~~~~~~~~~~

~~~~~~~~~~~

W ork is the
curse of the
drinking class, so
don't work unless
it is absolutely
necessary.

~~~~~~~~~~~

If somebody says
you have a problem
with ignorance and
apathy, just say,
"I don't know,
and I don't give
a shit."

Don't
trust nothin'
except
your instinct.

~~~~~~~~~~

Try not
to forget your
telephone number.

~~~~~~~~~~

When
you are feelin'
really down,
read the
Book of Job,
and see what
that sombitch
had to go
through!

~~~~~~~~~~

~~~~~~~~~

Do not sweat
the small stuff;
for that matter,
do not sweat
at all,
as it will
save you
money
on deodorant.

~~~~~~~~~

~~~~~~

D o not
buy stuff
you cannot afford,
unless you
really want to.

~~~~~~

~~~~~~~~~~

Ignorance
is the key
to everything
in life.
An ignorant
person is
constantly
surprised.

~~~~~~~~~~

~~~~~~~~

P eople say
the earth is round.
But you don't
have to believe it
if you don't
want to.

~~~~~~~~

~~~~~~~~

B ein'
a idiot is
a lot of fun
when ain't
nobody
lookin'.

~~~~~~~~

~~~~~~~~~~

Coach
Bear Bryant
was always fair.
He treated
every one of
us like trash.

~~~~~~~~~~

~~~~~~~~~~

Mama Gump
used to say:
"Rape, riot, and
revolution give rise
to prostitution
when *sonofabitch*
becomes a
household word."

~~~~~~~~~~

Y ou get into a
fight, first thing you do is
whang yourself over the
head with a fryin' pan
or somethin'.
Usually, your opponent
will then run away,
figgerin' that if you
was willing to do that
to *yourself*, then what
was you fixin'
to do to *him!*

~~~~~~~~~~

Do not wear T-shirts which advertise somebody else's products.

~~~~~~~~~~

~~~~~~~~

If you put
your money where
your mouth is,
you will look
very strange to
other people.

~~~~~~~~

~~~~~~~~~

Rules are
made to be
followed, but
there are
exceptions to all
rules—and I am
one of them.

~~~~~~~~~

~~~~~~~~~~

When you
go fishin', never
keep the little
fish. You won't
eat them, and the
big fish will.

~~~~~~~~~~

When you're
goin' frontwards,
watch in front.
When you're backin' up
watch in back.
And look
every which way
when you cross
the street.

~~~~~~~~~

Some people,
like me, are born
idiots, but
many more
become stupider
as they
go along.

~~~~~~~~~

~~~~~~~~~

If you
see a guy
beatin' his dog,
whip his ass
on the spot.

~~~~~~~~~

~~~~~~~~~~

Keep
a vegetable
garden
with lots
of nice
tomatoes.

~~~~~~~~~~

~~~~~~~~~

Your chances
of winnin' the
lottery
get a lot better
if you buy
a ticket.

~~~~~~~~~

~~~~~~~~

Uncle Gump
used to give
this advice:
"Never
be no
Big-Ass Pete."

~~~~~~~~

~~~~~~~~~~

Learn the
infield fly rule:
this will give
you a good
perspective
on life.

~~~~~~~~~~

~~~~~~~

I f you are
hungry and broke,
make a stew . . .

~~~~~~~

H

. . . However,
do not eat such
things from pigs as:

1. Tripe.
2. Souse.
3. Sow's-ears sandwiches.
4. Pig knuckles.
5. Brains.
6. Snouts, eyes, or tails.

But always be polite when
you decline these; some
people find them tasty.

~~~~~~~~

Don't be no
Ant-Man.
An Ant-Man
has very low
horizons.

~~~~~~~~

~~~~~~~~~

If you don't
know where
you are goin',
you will probably
not wind up
there.

~~~~~~~~~

~~~~~~~~~~~

Nobody
ever went
broke sayin'
''good mornin' ''
to folks.

~~~~~~~~~~~

~~~~~~~~~~

Life
must of been
a lot simpler
when the Indians
ran this country.

~~~~~~~~~~

~~~~~~~~~

Some people
you can dress up
in a $800 suit
and they look like
a million bucks;
me,
I still look
like a bozo.

~~~~~~~~~

~~~~~~~~

I t is one thing
to talk
bullshit;
it is another
to believe it.

~~~~~~~~

Don't
take any
wooden
Indians.

~~~~~~~~~~

If you can't
stand the heat,
get out of
the oven.

‿‿‿‿‿‿‿

Ἰf you
don't like it,
leave—and don't
let the doorknob
hit you in the ass
on the way out.

‿‿‿‿‿‿‿

I f you can't see the bottom, jump in, don't dive.

~~~~~~~~~~~~

D on't poke sticks at the monkeys.

~~~~~~~~

Honesty
is the best policy
unless
you are a crook.

~~~~~~~~

Mediocrity
killed
the cat.

~~~~~~~~~

Only laugh
when somethin'
is funny.

~~~~~~~~

Never
wear a belt
and suspenders
at the same time;
people might
think you are
paranoid.

~~~~~~~~

~~~~~~~~~~

Always be able
to look back
and say
"At least I
didn't lead no
humdrum life."

~~~~~~~~~~